CH

MAY   2006

Whales and Dolphins

KINGFISHER

a Houghton Mifflin Company imprint
222 Berkeley Street
Boston, Massachusetts 02116
www.houghtonmifflinbooks.com

First published in 2005
2 4 6 8 10 9 7 5 3 1

1TR/0105/PROSP/RNB(RNB)/140MA/F

LIBRARY OF CONGRESS CATALOGING-IN-PUBLICATION DATA
Harris, Caroline, 1964–
Whales and dolphins/Caroline Harris.—1st ed.
p. cm.—(Kingfisher young knowledge)
Includes index.
1. Cetacea—Juvenile literature. I. Title. II. Series.
QL737.C4H295 2005
599.5—dc22
2004018726

ISBN 0-7534-5869-1
ISBN 978-07534-5869-3

Printed in China

Senior editor: Carron Brown
Coordinating editor: Stephanie Pliakas
Designer: Joanne Brown
Cover designer: Poppy Jenkins
Picture manager: Cee Weston-Baker
DTP coordinator: Carsten Lorenz
DTP operator: Primrose Burton
Artwork archivist: Wendy Allison
Production controller: Jessamy Oldfield

Acknowledgments
The publishers would like to thank the following for permission to reproduce their material. Every care has been taken
to trace copyright holders. However, if there have been unintentional omissions or failure to trace copyright holders,
we apologize and will, if informed, endeavor to make corrections in any future edition.
b = bottom, c = center, l = left, t = top, r = right

Photographs: Cover Seapics/Doug Perrine; 1 Seapics/Masa Ushioda; 2–3 Getty/Taxi; 4–5 Nature pl/Brandon Cole; 6 Minden/Flip Nicklin;
7t Seapics/Armin Maywald; 7b Seapics/Doug Perrine; 8–9 Seapics/Doug Perrine; 8b Nature pl/Sue Flood; 9b Seapics/Ingrid Visser;
10 Minden/Flip Nicklin; 11t Seapics/David B. Fleetham; 11c Seapics/Mark Conlin; 11b OSF/David Fleetham; 12b Seapics/Michael S. Nolan;
13t Minden/Mitsuaki Iwago; 14–15 Corbis/Craig Tuttle; 15t Seapics/Doug Perrine; 15r Corbis/Lester V. Bergman; 15b Seapics/Doug Perrine;
16–17 Alamy; 17t Seapics/Hiroya Minakuchi; 17b Seapics/Masa Ushioda; 18–19 Seapics/Duncan Murrell; 19t Seapics/Philip Colla;
20–21 Minden/Flip Nicklin; 20b Ardea; 22–23 SeaQuest; 23b Seapics; 24–25 Minden/Flip Nicklin; 25t Seapics/Masa Ushioda;
25b Seapics/Xavier Safont; 26b Seapics/Hiroya Minakuchi; 26–27 Seapics/Masa Ushioda; 27t Seapics/Robert L. Pitman;
28b Seapics/James D. Watt; 29t Seapics/Bob Cranston; 30–31 Seapics/Doug Perrine; 31t Seapics/James D. Watt;
31b Seapics/Masa Ushioda; 32–33 Seapics; 32b Seapics/Hiroya Minakuchi; 33t Seapics/John K. B. Ford; 34 Minden/Flip Nicklin;
35t Corbis; 35b AA; 36–37 SeaQuest; 36c Corbis/Peter Turnley; 38–39 Seapics/Phillip Colla; 39t Minden/Flip Nicklin;
39b Minden/Flip Nicklin; 40–41 Minden/Mike Parry; 41 Corbis; 49 Minden/Flip Nicklin

Commissioned photography on pages 42–47 by Andy Crawford
Project maker and photo shoot coordinator: Miranda Kennedy
Thank you to models Lewis Manu, Adam Dyer, and Rebecca Roper.

Kingfisher Young Knowledge

Whales and Dolphins

Caroline Harris

KINGFISHER
BOSTON

Contents

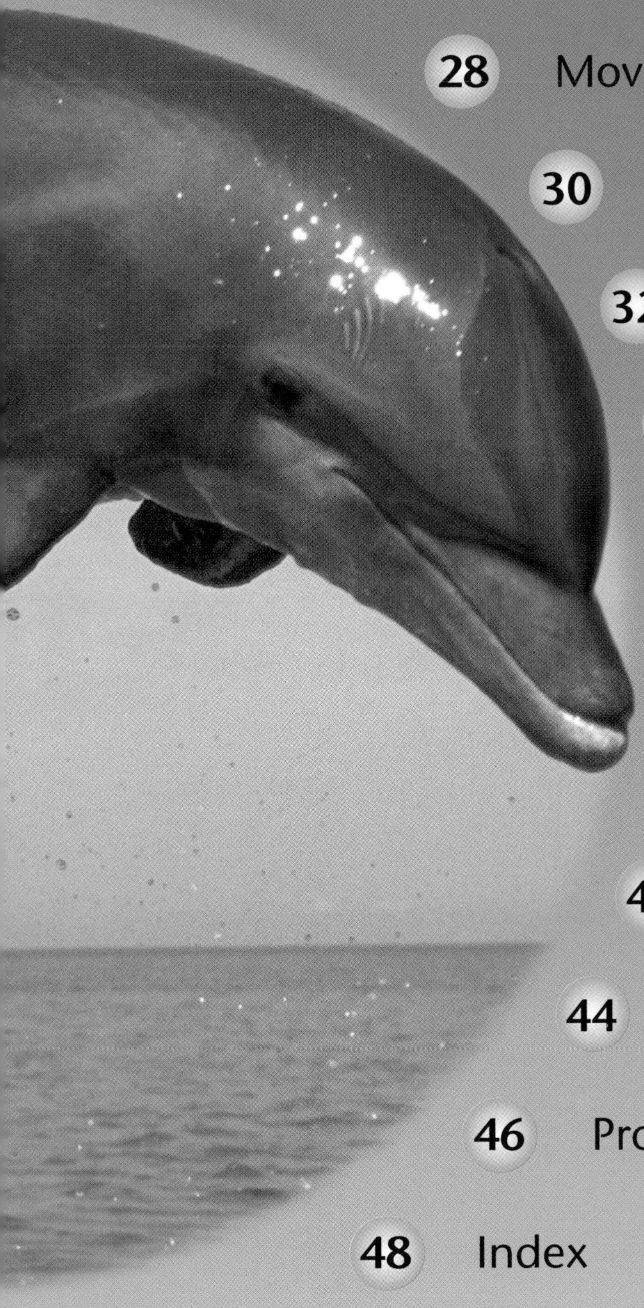

What are whales and dolphins?

Whales and dolphins are mammals that live in water. They have warm blood and have to swim to the ocean's surface in order to breathe.

Baby care

A dolphin mother usually gives birth to one baby at a time—called a calf. The newborn calf swims close to its mother's side for the first few weeks of its life.

mammals—warm-blooded animals that feed milk to their young

Bristly faces

Most mammals are covered with hair or fur. This porpoise's skin is smooth, but young cetaceans and some adults still have hairs on their faces.

Ripe old age

Dolphins can live up to 50 years old, while large whales, such as this southern right whale, may live to be 100!

cetaceans (say "si-tay-shiens")—group name for whales, dolphins, and porpoises

All around the world

There are more than 80 types of whales, dolphins, and porpoises. They live all over the world— in freezing oceans, tropical seas, and even in rivers.

Icy white

The beluga is also called the white whale. It makes its home in the very cold Arctic seas around Canada, Alaska, and Russia.

tropical—a hot, dry area close to the equator

Whales everywhere
Sperm whales live in every ocean. The females and young stay in tropical areas, while the males travel as far as the Arctic and Antarctic in order to feed.

Warm-water swimmer
The short-beaked common dolphin is found in many oceans and seas. It likes warm water, so it does not swim too far north or south.

Amazing creatures

Whales and dolphins come in many incredible shapes and sizes. Do you know that the largest animal on Earth is a whale?

Dolphin magic

The boto, or Amazon river dolphin, is one of four species of dolphins that are found only in rivers. It is also called the pink dolphin because it has rose-colored skin.

species—a group of animals or plants with the same features

Sea giant

The blue whale is the world's largest mammal. It can weigh 190 tons—the same as 32 elephants. A blue whale this big has a heart that is the size of a small car!

blue whale

skeleton of a blue whale

Water unicorn

The male narwhal has a tusk that can reach ten feet long. Tales of unicorns may have begun when people first saw narwhal tusks.

unicorn—*a mythical animal that looks like a horse with a long horn*

Ancient
whales

When the dinosaurs died out, mammals began to live in many different places. This is how whales and dolphins came to live in the oceans.

Digging up the past

We know about ancient cetaceans by studying the fossils and bones they left behind—such as this dolphin skull.

fossils—any evidence of living things from the past

Grass-eating cousins

Cows, sheep, whales, and dolphins share the same ancestor— an ancient mammal that lived on land and ate leaves.

Early whale

Basilosaurus lived 40 million years ago. Over a long period of time the land mammals that moved into the sea changed their shape in order to adapt to life in the water.

ancestor—an animal from which later animals have developed

Built for the sea

The smooth, long shape of cetaceans means that they are able to swim through water easily. Salty seawater is good at keeping heavy things buoyant, which is why whales can grow so large.

Full power

Instead of back legs, cetaceans have very strong tails with two flat paddles called flukes. Bottlenose dolphins can stand up just by using their tails alone.

buoyant—able to float in the water

dolphin flipper bones

human hand bones

Handy flippers

Cetaceans have flippers instead of front legs. When you look at these bones, you can see that a dolphin's flipper shape follows the same pattern as a hand.

Layers of blubber

This southern right whale has a layer of fat, called blubber, to keep out the cold. It helps whales survive in freezing water.

fat—the soft, oily part under the skin of an animal

Coming up for air

Like other mammals, whales and dolphins breathe using their lungs. This means that they come to the surface to take in fresh air and blow out used air.

Deep down
Most whales can stay underwater for half an hour before needing to take a breath. Cetaceans take in air through a blowhole on the top of their head.

lungs—the parts inside the body that are used for breathing

Blowing high

Many whales, such as this blue whale, have a double blowhole. The blowhole closes up when they dive so that water will not get in.

Unique spray

Dolphins have a single blowhole. The pattern of mist, called "blow," that sprays out is different for every species of cetacean.

blowhole—the airway that whales, dolphins, and porpoises breathe through

Filter **feeders**

Cetaceans are split into two groups: those that have teeth and those that do not. The toothless whales, known as baleen whales, include humpbacks and grays. They feed by filtering tiny marine animals and small fish from the sea.

filtering—*collecting tiny objects from the liquid in which they are floating*

What is baleen?

Instead of teeth, toothless whales have baleen—stiff, hairy sheets that hang in rows from their top jaws. Baleen traps food as water is filtered through it.

Big eaters

To eat enough, humpbacks gulp huge mouthfuls of water. Folds in their necks expand like a balloon in order to let in even more water.

marine—from the sea

Clever hunters

All dolphins, porpoises, and more than half of whale species have teeth. They eat fish and larger sea creatures. Sperm whales love to eat giant squid.

Fearless predators

The orca, often called the killer whale, is actually a large dolphin. Its diet includes sea lions and even other cetaceans.

predators—*animals that hunt and eat other animals*

Open wide

A dolphin's teeth are used for grabbing, not chewing. They swallow their prey whole.

Teamwork

Bottlenose dolphins often hunt together. They surround groups of fish, sometimes driving them onto land and coming halfway out of the water to grab them.

prey—*animals that are eaten by other animals*

Underwater senses

Whales and dolphins use hearing, sight, and touch in order to understand their world. They also have a special sense called echolocation.

Earplugs

The humpback whale does not have ears like ours. It has a tiny hole on both sides of its head that is closed by a plug of wax— this stops water from getting inside.

wax—an oily material inside the ear that protects it

What is echolocation?

Echolocation is used by dolphins to navigate and find prey. They make clicking noises that "bounce," or echo, off an object, telling them where it is and what it is like.

Clear vision

They may have small eyes, but most cetaceans can see well. A thick, greasy liquid stops the eyes from becoming sore in the salty water.

navigate—to find your way around

Sea songs

All cetaceans use sounds to communicate. Baleen whales make low sounds, from loud grunts and squeals to gurgling noises. Dolphins whistle, squeak, and click.

Noisy neighbors

Dolphins make different noises for different reasons. Jaw clapping, which involves opening and shutting their mouths, is a sign that there may be a fight on the way.

communicate—to send a message to another creature

The latest tune

Male humpbacks sing patterns of notes and sounds that can last up to half an hour.

Brain power

Dolphins have large brains in relation to the size of their bodies. They are fast learners and can even understand simple sentences.

brain—*the body part inside the head that is used to learn and to think*

Playing with waves

From slapping their fins and tails on the water's surface to spinning in the air, cetaceans display all types of behavior both above and below the water.

High fliers

Dusky dolphins are among the most acrobatic of all dolphins. They do breathtaking leaps and somersaults.

behavior—how animals act

Who's there?

Orcas spyhop, sticking
their heads straight
up out of the water,
to spot penguins
and seals on the ice.

Amazing sight

When whales
launch themselves
out of the sea, it is called
breaching. Humpbacks have
been seen breaching 100
times, over and over again.

acrobatic—doing movements that are difficult and skillful

Moving along

Whales migrate, or travel, between cold seas in the summer—where there is plenty of food—and warmer waters in the winter—where they have their babies.

Record holders

Humpbacks and grays make the longest journeys. They can swim up to 10,000 miles in one year.

North America

South America

breeding ground—where animals go to find a mate and have their young

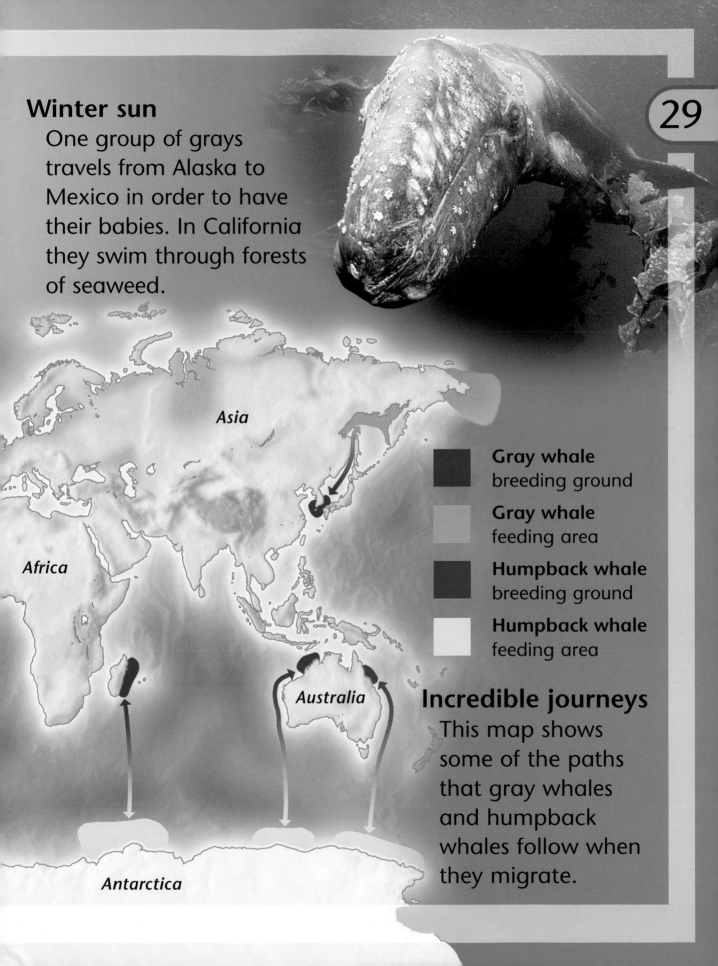

Winter sun

One group of grays travels from Alaska to Mexico in order to have their babies. In California they swim through forests of seaweed.

Asia

Africa

Australia

Antarctica

Gray whale breeding ground

Gray whale feeding area

Humpback whale breeding ground

Humpback whale feeding area

Incredible journeys

This map shows some of the paths that gray whales and humpback whales follow when they migrate.

30 New lives

Whale and dolphin babies swim as soon as they are born, but it takes many years until a calf is an adult.

Big babies

A humpback calf can measure one third of its mother's length when it is born! It will feed on her milk for the first 11 months of its life.

pregnancy—the time when a baby grows inside of its mother

Long pregnancy
Dolphins can be pregnant for more than one year. The actual birth, however, is quick and may be over in less than one hour.

Staying close
Cetacean mothers stay close to their calves so that they can protect them from predators.

Social animals

A group of cetaceans is known as a pod. Many pods are related, while others come together to feed or to protect their young.

Family ties

All of the members of an orca pod are related to one original mother or grandmother. Orcas usually stay with their family for life.

social—living in a group

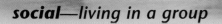

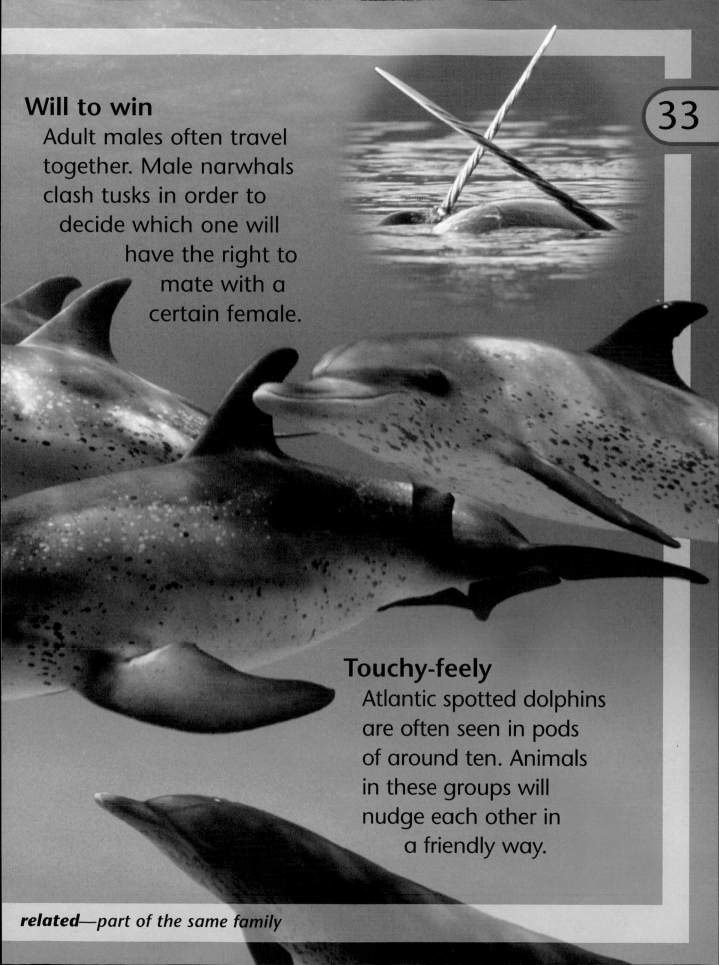

Will to win

Adult males often travel together. Male narwhals clash tusks in order to decide which one will have the right to mate with a certain female.

Touchy-feely

Atlantic spotted dolphins are often seen in pods of around ten. Animals in these groups will nudge each other in a friendly way.

related—*part of the same family*

Making friends

People have always thought of dolphins as friendly creatures. Whales were once thought of as monsters, but today we want to protect them.

Watery friends

Swimming with dolphins has become popular with adults and children. Dolphins will even help people who are in trouble in the sea.

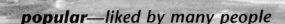

popular—liked by many people

Ancient links

This painting of dolphins is on a wall of the Palace of Knossos on the Greek island of Crete. It is 3,500 years old.

Big books

There are many stories about giant whales. In the Bible Jonah was swallowed by a whale—and survived.

Human dangers

Some things people do can harm cetaceans. For a long time whales have been hunted for their meat, baleen, and blubber. Fishnets and pollution are also dangers.

Whale rescue

Many dolphins and whales get caught and can die in fishnets. This tangled-up sperm whale is being freed by a diver.

Under threat

The Yangtze river in China is home to the baiji. This dolphin is endangered because the river is full of pollution.

endangered—*in danger of dying out*

Whaling ban
Whale hunting—known as whaling—has killed millions of cetaceans. Most countries have agreed to stop completely.

pollution—*harmful waste material*

Growing knowledge

The more we discover about whales and dolphins, the more amazing we find that they are. It is important to know as much as we can about them so that they can be better protected.

Getting to know them

Researchers can identify individual Risso's dolphins from the scars on their bodies. The pattern on each dolphin's body is different.

scars—marks left on the skin after cuts have healed

Satellite tagging

Cetaceans can now
be followed from space!
The tag on this beluga
sends information
to a satellite, which
can then track down
where the beluga is.

satellite—a spacecraft that travels around and around Earth

Looking and learning

There are chances to watch whales, dolphins, and porpoises in the wild throughout the world, from Ireland to the Caribbean and from Canada to Australia.

Free to roam

Today there are a few cetacean sanctuaries. It is hoped that in the future there will be even more.

sanctuaries—safe places that are protected from damage by humans

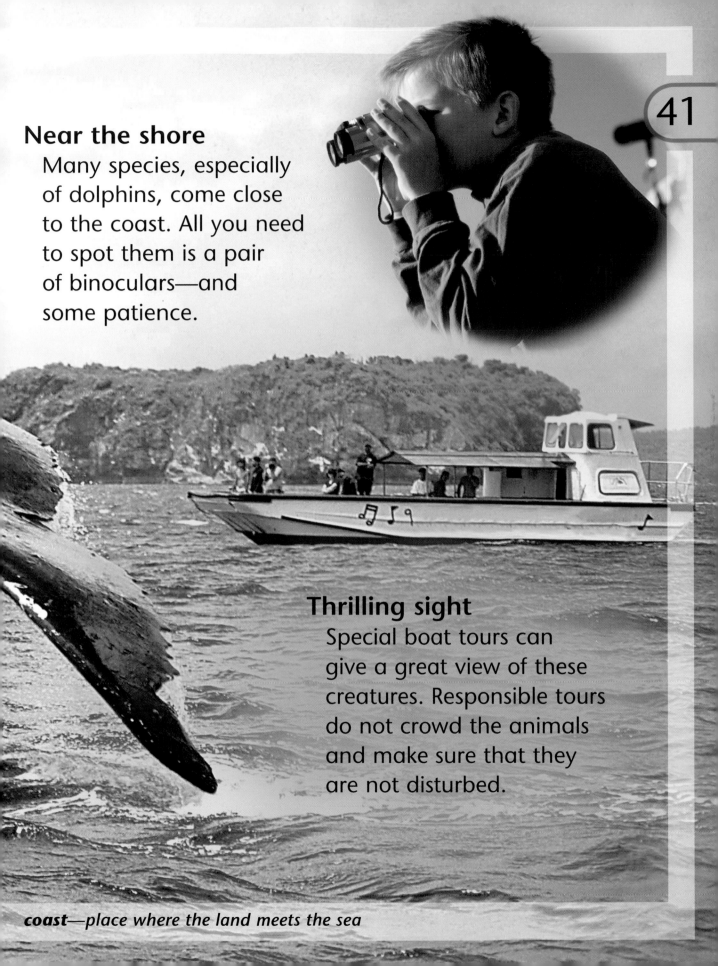

Near the shore

Many species, especially of dolphins, come close to the coast. All you need to spot them is a pair of binoculars—and some patience.

Thrilling sight

Special boat tours can give a great view of these creatures. Responsible tours do not crowd the animals and make sure that they are not disturbed.

coast—place where the land meets the sea

Dolphin mobile

Leaping high

Hang this mobile in your bedroom, and you will have dolphins dancing before your eyes. Shiny paper makes them sparkle in the light.

You will need

- Pencil
- Tracing paper
- Thin cardboard
- Scissors
- Modeling clay
- Compass
- Foil/shiny paper
- Glue
- Ruler
- Ribbon
- Thick cardboard (12 in. x 12 in.)

dolphin template

Decorate each dolphin with foil or shiny paper.

1 Trace the template and transfer the shape onto thin cardboard. Do this five times so you have five dolphins. Cut out the dolphins.

2 Place modeling clay under the top fin of each dolphin shape. Using a compass, make a hole in each fin as shown.

Draw a line from the bottom-left corner of the thick cardboard to the top-right corner using a ruler. Cut along the line to make two triangles and then decorate them.

Cut a notch halfway down the peak of one triangle. Cut a notch halfway up from the bottom of the other triangle. Make holes at the ends of each triangle.

dolphin mobile

Slot the triangles together to form a hanger. Make a hole where the two triangles meet at the bottom and another hole at the top.

Use ribbon to attach each dolphin to the hanger and then fasten the knots. Pull ribbon through the hole at the top of the hanger to make a loop. You can now hang up your mobile.

Whale bookmark

Intelligent creatures

Cetaceans are among the smartest of all animals. Make bookmarks in the shape of sea mammals to hold your place in your favorite books.

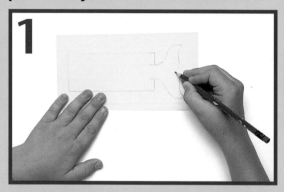

On a piece of white construction paper measure a 2 in. x 6 in. rectangle. Draw a whale's tail at one short end of the shape. Draw waves where the tail meets the sea.

You will need

- White construction paper
- Ruler
- Pencil
- Scissors
- Blue holographic paper
- Glue
- Markers
- Glitter pens

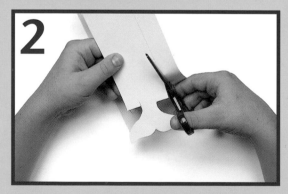

Cut out the bookmark, being careful to cut around the shape of the whale's tail and around the top of the waves.

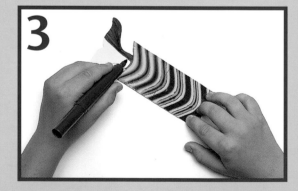

Glue blue holographic paper to both sides of the bookmark for the sea. Use markers and glitter pens to color in the tail.

Does it float?

Testing buoyancy

When you put different items in water, some float on the surface, and others sink to the bottom. Whales and dolphins need to come up for air, so they have to be bouyant enough not to sink straight down.

You will need
- Large, clear bowl
- Water
- Apple
- Pebble
- Cork
- Ice cube

1 Examine the apple, pebble, cork, and ice cube. Will they float, or will they sink?

2 One by one, put each item into a bowl of water—were you right about which would float and which would sink?

Sea giants

Blue whales are the biggest animals on Earth. They can reach 100 feet long, which is the size of a large swimming pool. This project will give you an idea of just how large they are.

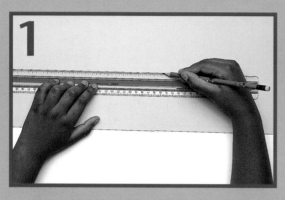

Using a ruler, measure and mark a 12 in. space, then a 1 in. space, a 3 in. space, another 1 in. space, and, finally, a 2 in. space on the poster board.

You will need

- Long piece of poster board
- Ruler
- Pencil
- Paints
- Paintbrush
- Tissue paper: green, blue, red
- Glue
- Cotton balls
- Scissors
- Gold holographic paper

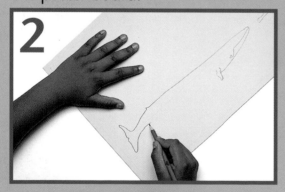

Draw a blue whale from tail to head in the 12 in. space. Then draw an orca in the 3 in. space and an elephant in the 2 in. space.

Paint the blue whale, orca, and elephant, copying the colors and markings shown on the final picture on the opposite page.

4

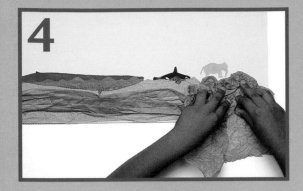

Decorate the picture with strips of tissue paper: green for land under the elephant and blue for the sea around the orca and whale.

5

Glue on cotton balls for clouds. Then cut out a circle and eight strips of gold holographic paper and glue them down to make a sun.

To finish your picture, twist some red tissue paper and glue it down to create a border. Now you can see how big a blue whale really is!

Index